W9-ARG-914

Step-by-Step
Origami

Clive Stevens

Heinemann Library
Chicago, Illinois

© 2003 Reed Educational & Professional Publishing
Published by Heinemann Library,
an imprint of Reed Educational & Professional Publishing,
Chicago, Illinois

Customer Service 888-454-2279

Visit our website at www.heinemannlibrary.com

Photographs and design copyright © Search Press Limited, 2002
Text copyright © Clive Stevens 2002
Photographs by Charlotte de la Bédoyère,
Search Press Studios
Designed by Search Press
Printed in Italy by L.E.G.O.

07 06 05 04 03
10 9 8 7 6 5 4 3 2 1

Library of Congress Cataloging-in-Publication Data

Stevens, Clive, 1947-
     Origami / Clive Stevens.
     p.cm.--(Step-by-Step)
Includes index
Contents: Materials--Techniques--Origami bases--Layered fan--Secrets envelope--Paper penguin--Picture frame--Japanese card--Obi bookmark--Folded flower--Space rocket--Flapping bird--Blow-up box.
ISBN 1-40340-699-5 (HC), 1-40340-716-9 (Pbk)
1. Origami--Juvenile literature. [1. Origami. 2. Handicraft] I. Title.
TT870. S7297 2002
736'.982--dc21

                                        2002027325

Acknowledgments

The author and publishers are grateful to the following for permission to reproduce copyright material: Robin Macey, page 5.

Every effort has been made to contact copyright holders of any material reproduced in this book. Any omissions will be rectified in subsequent printings if notice is given to the publisher.

To my dear Sue for her endless patience, and to Sarah and Tom who I know will enjoy these projects.

Some words are shown in bold, **like this**. You can find out what they mean by looking in the glossary.

Contents

Introduction

It is generally believed that paper was invented in China around the first century **C.E.** and the Chinese soon began to fold the new material into decorative shapes. When paper was introduced to Japan in the sixth century C.E. by **Buddhist** monks, it rapidly became an important part of their culture. Paper was used as part of many religious **ceremonies,** and even as a building material. The Japanese turned paper folding into an art, and in Japan it is as important as painting and sculpture. Origami comes from the Japanese words for folding, *ori*, and paper, *kami.*

The Japanese passed on their paper folding designs by word of mouth; many were passed down from mother to daughter. In the early days, paper was too expensive to be used for fun, so paper folding was done only for important ceremonies. Paper butterflies were made to decorate the *sake* (rice wine) cups used at Japanese weddings.

By the seventeenth century, paper had become less expensive, and origami had become a popular pastime in Japan. The first origami books with diagrams and instructions were published in the early eighteenth century.

Today, master paper folders can be found all over the world. Folding techniques have improved so much that they would have astounded the ancient Japanese who invented origami.

In this book, you will learn how to make good, crisp folds so that your paper will hold the right shapes. Follow the instructions carefully, and this is all you will need to know to make some simple but very interesting projects.

In origami, many different shapes can be made from a few simple **bases.** The Origami Bases chapter on pages 10 and 11 shows you how to make two of these bases. Once you have mastered folding them, you are ready to make some very impressive projects!

Don't worry if your folding does not work the first time. Go over the instructions and pictures again carefully, and you will soon find where you went wrong.

You hardly need any materials to do origami, and it is easy to become hooked. After a few tries, you will learn the folds by heart. Then, all you will need is a piece of paper to produce designs that will amaze your friends!

Opposite
This amazing origami beetle is only about 1 in. (2.5cm) long. It was designed and folded by the Italian paper folder, Alfredo Giunta.

Designed and folded by Alfredo Giunta. Photograph by Robin Macey.

Materials

Origami is the best known of all the paper crafts. The rules of origami do not allow the paper to be cut, glued or decorated. It may only be folded. For this reason, very little equipment is required.

Paper is the most important thing to start with! When practicing origami, use simple white paper that is made for computer printers. It is not expensive to buy in large amounts, and can be used for most origami designs. However, for the projects in this book, colored paper will look best.

You can use *paper* of many different types, colors and thicknesses for origami. You can also use thin posterboard. *Patterned paper* such as *gift wrapping paper* is ideal for some projects. *Origami paper* can be bought in craft shops. It comes in packs containing various sizes and is usually colored on one side and white on the other. It is thinner than standard printer paper and a little stronger. It is best for two-tone models such as the Paper Penguin project on pages 16–17. *Metallic paper* can be very effective for projects such as the Space Rocket on pages 26–27. It is metallic on one side and white on the other, and can be bought from art and craft stores.

A *long ruler* is useful for measuring paper before cutting it to the right size.

Scissors are used only for cutting paper to size. Paper is not cut in origami once the shape is folded.

An *ordinary ruler* can be used to create a fold, as in the Paper Penguin project on pages 16–17.

A *pencil* or a *toothpick* can be used to curl the edges of paper for a finishing touch, as in the Folded Flower project on pages 24–25.

For some projects such as the Obi Bookmark on pages 22–23, you will need to cut strips out of *large pieces of paper*. These sheets are 16½ in. x 23 in. (42cm x 59cm).

Techniques

Folding in half

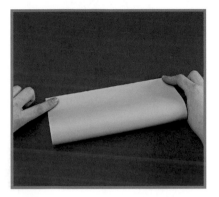

 1 Fold the bottom corners upward to meet the top corners. This will make a **horizontal** fold.

2 Make a crease in the middle. Press and slide your finger from the middle to the edge, and then from the middle to the other edge. Be sure the corners stay together.

3 Make the crease tighter by pressing and sliding your fingernail along it.

Folding diagonally

Start with a square piece of paper. Lift one corner and match it up with the corner **diagonally** opposite to it. Make a crease in the middle of the paper and press it from the middle to the sides. This makes a diagonal fold.

Folding at an angle

Lay a strip of paper horizontally. Fold part of the strip downward so that the edges of the strip make a right angle, like the corner of a square.

Reverse Folding (internal)

Reverse folding means that you push a fold until it folds in the opposite direction. A valley fold (which dips downward) becomes a mountain fold (which points upward), and vice versa. This internal reverse fold is used for the Flapping Bird project on pages 28–29.

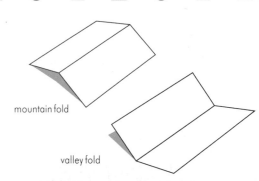

mountain fold

valley fold

1 Fold a square piece of paper in half diagonally. Fold the top corner down as shown and crease it sharply.

2 Open the paper slightly. Pull the top point toward you. Reverse the mountain fold in the middle of the point, making it a valley fold.

3 Remake the diagonal fold and open it slightly to show the point with its valley fold.

Reverse Folding (external)

This type of external reverse fold is used for the Paper Penguin project on pages 16–17.

1 Take a square piece of paper and fold it diagonally. Fold down the top point as shown and crease firmly.

2 Open it with the diagonal mountain fold facing toward you. Fold the top point toward you. Reverse the fold in the middle of the point. Now remake the diagonal fold, so that the point comes down on the outside of the diagonal fold.

Origami Bases

Many origami designs come from a few simple **bases.** Here are two bases that can lead to all sorts of different projects.

Bird Base

This base is used to make the Flapping Bird project on page 28. Steps 1 to 3 are also used in the Folded Flower project on page 24.

1 Take a square of piece of paper. Fold it **diagonally.** Crease it firmly and open. Fold on the other diagonal, crease and open it. Turn the paper over so that your diagonal folds are mountain folds, as shown above.

2 Now fold up the bottom two corners to meet the top two corners and fold the paper in half **horizontally.** Crease, unfold, and then fold the paper **vertically** to make a cross shape. Turn the paper over and place it as shown, so that the horizontal and vertical folds are mountain folds, and the diagonal folds are valley folds that dip down.

3 Hold the edges of the horizontal fold as shown. Move your hands downward until the paper forms a square. Flip one corner to the other side so that there are two flaps on each side of the square as shown.

open end

10

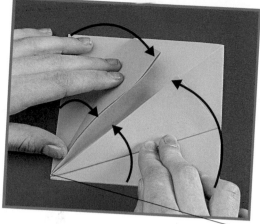

open end

open end

4 Fold the front flaps, lining up the edges with the middle crease. Make sure the open end of the shape is at the bottom as shown.

5 Turn over and do the same thing on the other side.

Rocket Base

This base is used in the Space Rocket project on pages 26–27 and in the Blow-up Box on pages 30–31.

1

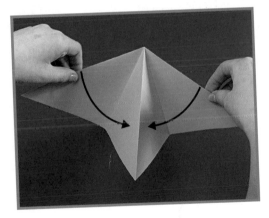

Start making the Bird Base, but only go as far as Step 2. Turn the paper over so that the diagonal folds are mountain folds and the horizontal folds are valley folds. Pinch the corners of one of the diagonal folds. Bring your hands together to form a triangle.

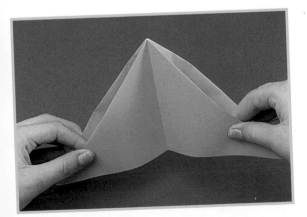

2

Flip one corner to the other side. The triangle should now have two flaps on each side, like the square made in step 3 of the Bird Base.

Note If your origami bases have not turned out right, check these things.
• Make sure your folds are sharply creased.
• If your diagonal folds are mountain folds, your horizontal folds should be valley folds.
• Make sure the open end of the shape is at the bottom.

Layered Fan

Many people have learned to make a simple fan by folding a piece of paper into a **concertina** shape. This type of paper fan may have been your first introduction to paper folding! However, folding this way can lead to uneven folds and a messy finished fan. The origami fan in this project is made from basic valley and mountain folds. With this method you fold the paper so that it is divided equally.

YOU WILL NEED
Three different colored papers:
4 in. x 11¾ in. (10cm x 30cm)
4¾ in. x 11¾ in. (12cm x 30cm)
5½ in. x 11¾ in. (14cm x 30cm)

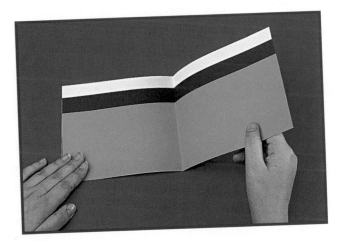

 Place all three pieces of paper together as shown. Fold them in half and unfold.

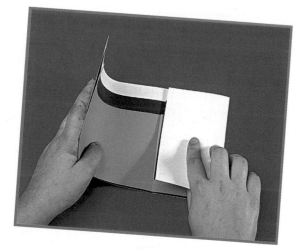

 Fold the right and left edges in, lining up the edges with the center line.

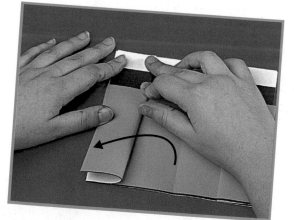

3 Take one of the edges that you have folded into the middle, and fold it back to the new edge. Repeat on the other side.

4 Fold the whole shape in half, bringing the double outside edges together.

5 Fold the top flap back, lining up the edge with the outside fold. Turn the paper over and do the same thing on the other side.

6 Open the set of papers and pinch the folds at the bottom together to form a multicolored fan.

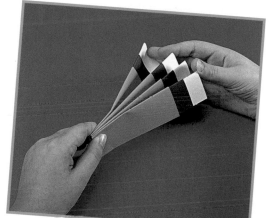

FURTHER IDEAS

Make fans from patterned origami paper, wrapping paper, or even beautiful Japanese handmade papers.

Secrets Envelope

This handy envelope is made using simple folds as well as a tuck fold. It can be any size you want, from a tiny purse for loose change, to an envelope like the one shown here, for large secrets. Remember that the envelope you end up with will be much smaller than the piece of paper you start with. You need to cut down a 16½ in. x 23 in. (42cm x 59cm) piece of paper to make an envelope as big as the one shown here. What you hide in your secrets envelope is up to you!

YOU WILL NEED
Colored or patterned paper
12 in. x 20 in. (30cm x 50cm)

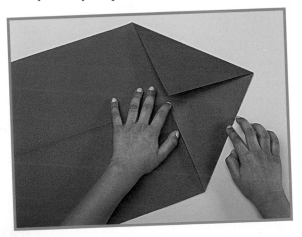

1 Place the paper shiny side down and fold it in half **horizontally.** Unfold it. Fold the two top corners in to the center line.

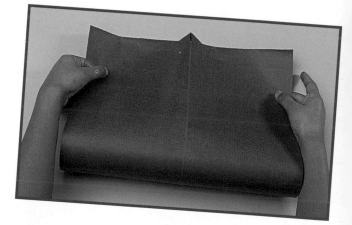

2 Fold the bottom edge up to the point at the top.

 3

Now fold the outside edges in to the center fold.

14

 4

Fold the bottom edge to the top of the **diagonal** folds.

 5

Tuck the flap into the front pocket.

 6

Fold the point down to form the front flap of the secrets envelope.

FURTHER IDEAS

Try using metallic or patterned papers, or decorate a piece of paper yourself using paints or felt tip markers before folding.

Paper Penguin

Origami paper with black on one side and white on the other works perfectly for this project. Using very few folds, you can create something that stands up like a real penguin. Penguins are some of the most sociable of all birds—they like to swim and eat in groups.

YOU WILL NEED

A 4 in. (10cm) square piece of paper, black on one side and white on the other.

 Fold the paper in half **diagonally** with the white on the inside to make a crease. Unfold it. Turn the paper over. Take a corner at one end of the diagonal fold, and fold it up 1 in. (2.5cm) as shown. Crease sharply.

 Reverse the diagonal fold so that the white is on the outside, to make the shape as shown.

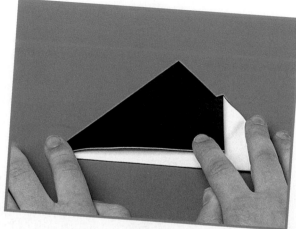

 Fold the top point down so the long edge is ½ in. (1.5cm) from the bottom fold. Crease. Turn the paper over and repeat. This step is like making the wings on a paper airplane.

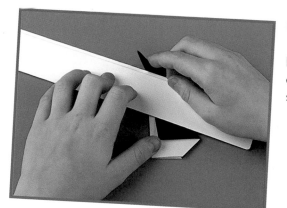

Place a ruler over the shape and fold the point down against the edge of a ruler at the angle shown. Remove the ruler and crease.

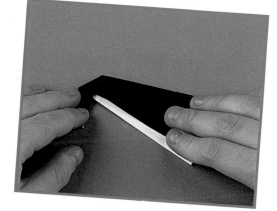

5

Open up slightly and pull the point toward you, making an external reverse fold as shown on page 9. This will make the penguin's head point downward.

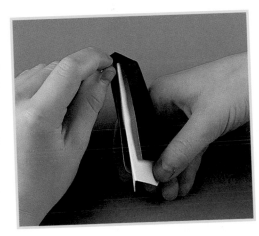

Crease the penguin again so that it is completely flat. Open it up to reveal the finished penguin.

FURTHER IDEAS

Make a group of penguins in different colors and sizes. You could even make a paper pool for them to dive into!

Picture Frame

This simple origami frame is the perfect place to put one of your drawings or a favorite photograph. Use thin posterboard instead of paper to make a strong frame. The picture that goes inside this frame can be up to 5¾ in. (14.5cm) square, but don't forget that only a 4 in. (10.5cm) square in the middle will show.

YOU WILL NEED
Square of brightly colored thin posterboard,
11¾ in. x 11¾ in.
(30cm x 30cm)

 Fold the square in half **diagonally.**

 Open the paper and fold it in half diagonally the other way.

Open it again. Your diagonal folds should be valley folds. Fold all four corners down to the center. The points should almost touch each other.

 4

Turn the paper over and again fold all of the corners to the center.

 5

Turn the square over and fold the four points out to their corners.

 6

Measure your picture frame. Draw a picture or find a photograph this size. Remember that the corners will be hidden by the frame. Slide the picture into the frame.

FURTHER IDEAS

Fold only as far as step 4 to make a coaster. Cover it in plastic to make it spill-proof.

Japanese Card

People have been sending one another greeting cards for hundreds of years. The first ones celebrated holidays or religious festivals, but now they are sent for all kinds of reasons. Handmade cards are even more special than store-bought ones. This Japanese greeting card has contrasting shades of the same color to make it eye-catching. You can open the flaps and write your message inside.

YOU WILL NEED
Two pieces of contrasting colored paper, 9 in. (23.5cm) square

1 Put the squares of paper one on top of the other. Measure across the **diagonal** and mark it in thirds—every 4½ in. (11cm).

2 Fold the corner along the diagonal. Fold on your first mark. The point should touch your second mark.

3 Unfold. Turn the paper around and fold the opposite corner up so the point touches your first fold.

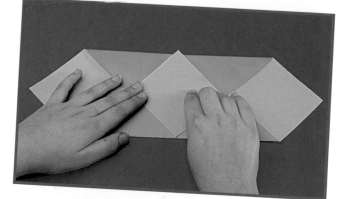

4

Fold the point down to the bottom. Refold the top corner along the crease. Fold the point up to the top edge.

5

Fold one side in to cover the light-colored square in the middle. Fold the other side in as well.

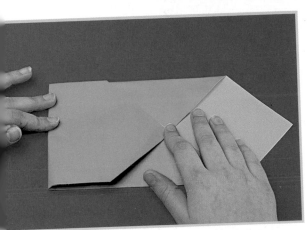

6

Fold the triangular flap out to the outside edge. Do the same thing on the other side.

FURTHER IDEAS

Create a traditional Japanese card from glossy black and red paper.

Obi Bookmark

This traditional folding technique looks like the sash, or *obi*, worn round a Japanese **kimono**. Use bright, contrasting colors to give your bookmark a modern look. You need to start with long strips of paper, so make sure you cut them from a 16½ in. x 23 in. (42cm x 59cm) size sheet. Once you have mastered the overlapping technique, you will be able to make a variety of bookmarks in different lengths and colors. They make the ideal gift for a friend who likes to read.

YOU WILL NEED

Two strips of paper in contrasting colors, 21¼ in. x 1¼ in. (54cm x 3cm)
Scissors
Ruler

10¼ in. (26cm) from the left

1

Put one strip on top of the other. Fold the strips at an angle, as shown on page 8. The fold should come 10¼ in. (26cm) from the left-hand end of the strips.

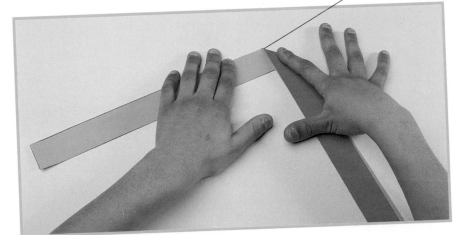

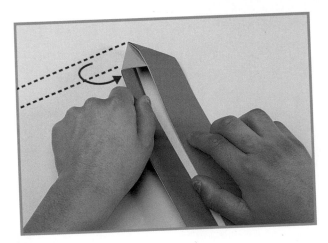

2 Fold the left-hand strips under at an angle. The strips should run **parallel** to the right-hand strips.

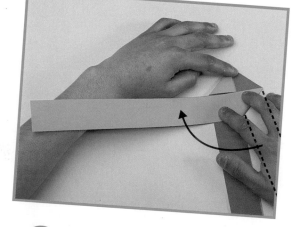

3 Fold the right-hand strips at an angle as shown.

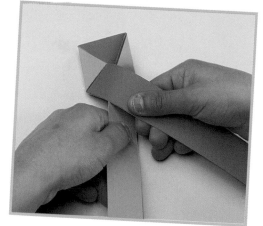

Slip the top right-hand strips under the left-hand strips.

Repeat steps 2, 3 and 4 until four squares have been formed.

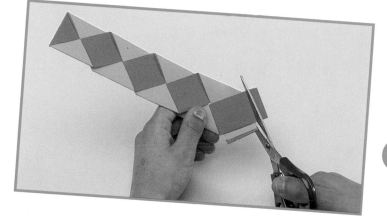

Fold the excess under neatly or trim the ends using scissors.

FURTHER IDEAS
Use different kinds of paper together. For example, try textured and glossy paper or patterned and plain paper.

Folded Flower

This origami flower starts as a square, but with a few folds it turns into a flower shape. Curling the ends of the petals gives it a natural beauty. Why not make lots of flowers in different colors, with straws or pipe cleaners for stems? Then you can arrange them in a vase or bouquet.

YOU WILL NEED
Square of brightly colored paper,
4 in. x 4 in. (10cm x 10cm)
Pencil or toothpick

1 Fold the square **diagonally**. Crease it firmly. Open it up and fold it on the other diagonal. Open up the paper as shown above. Your diagonal folds should be mountain folds.

2 Fold up the bottom two corners to meet the top two corners and make a **horizontal** fold. Crease, unfold, and then fold the paper in half the other way. Now your horizontal folds are mountain folds and your diagonal folds are valley folds.

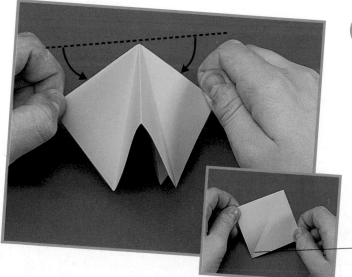

3 Hold the ends of a horizontal fold with both hands as shown. Move your hands together until the paper forms a square. There should be two flaps on each side.

open end

open end

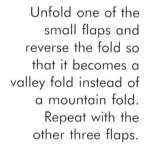

4 Turn the square so that the open point is at the top. Fold the front flaps as shown, bringing the edges together in the middle. Crease firmly. Turn over and do the same thing on the other side.

5

Unfold one of the small flaps and reverse the fold so that it becomes a valley fold instead of a mountain fold. Repeat with the other three flaps.

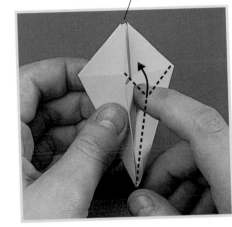

open end

6 Open the flower. Using a pencil or a toothpick, roll the tops of all four points down to create the curl of a petal.

FURTHER IDEAS

Make much bigger flowers. Then make smaller flowers without curling the petals. They can be the centers for the big flowers.

Space Rocket

This rocket is made from origami paper that is silver metallic on one side and white on the other. It has legs that point outward at an angle so it can stand up on its own, ready for take-off! Once you have mastered the Rocket Base, you are ready to fold and launch your own rocket—or maybe a whole fleet of spaceships!

YOU WILL NEED

Square of metallic paper, 8¼ in. x 8¼ in. (21cm x 21cm)

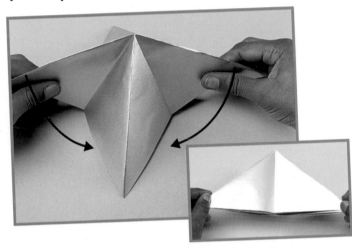

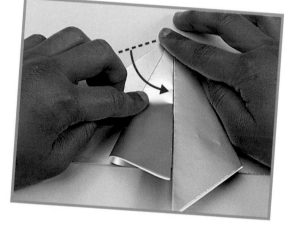

1 First make the Rocket **Base** as shown on page 11. Make sure that the shiny side of the paper is on the outside when you make your **diagonal** folds and on the inside when you make the **horizontal** folds. Hold the edges of a diagonal mountain fold and bring your hands in to make the triangle shape shown, with two flaps on each side.

2 Fold the outer edges in to the middle as shown. Turn the paper over and repeat.

3 Fold the outer corners to the middle. Turn the paper over and do the same thing on the other side.

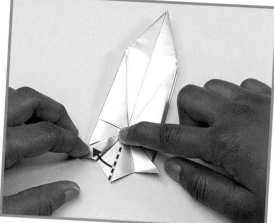

Fold the bottom
points out at an
angle as shown.

5

Turn over
and repeat
step 4.

6 Carefully open the
rocket by placing your
finger inside it and
lightly pressing out.

FURTHER IDEAS
Leave the rocket flat as in
step 5 and glue it to a
greeting card.

Flapping Bird

This bird is a variation of the traditional origami crane, a bird that is a Japanese symbol for peace. The crane is also the symbol for many international origami societies. This version is simpler, but if you hold it in the right place, it actually flaps its wings. Once you have gotten the hang of the Bird Base shown on pages 10 and 11, you will be ready to fold this impressive project to amaze all of your friends.

YOU WILL NEED
Square piece of paper,
9¾ in. x 9¾ in.
(24.5cm x 24.5cm)

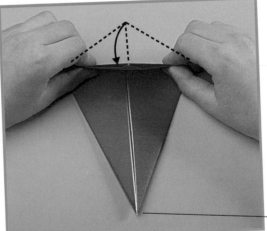

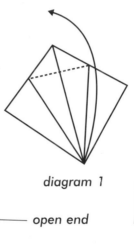

diagram 1

open end

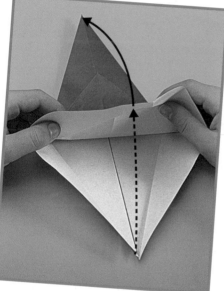

1 Start with the Bird **Base** shown on pages 10 and 11, with the open end at the bottom. Fold the smaller triangle down. Crease it and fold it back to its original position.

2 Unfold the side flaps as in diagram 1. Fold the bottom point up, covering the small triangle from step 1. The point should touch the top. Turn the paper over and repeat this step on the back to make the shape shown in diagram 2.

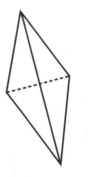

diagram 2

3 Fold the top flap on the right over to the left. Turn the paper over and repeat, folding only the top right flap to the left.

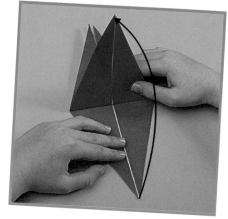

 4

Fold the bottom flap up. Turn the paper over and repeat.

5

Pull the hidden points in the middle out and down. Crease them in the position shown for the bird's head and tail.

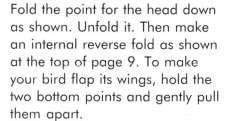 **6**

Fold the point for the head down as shown. Unfold it. Then make an internal reverse fold as shown at the top of page 9. To make your bird flap its wings, hold the two bottom points and gently pull them apart.

FURTHER IDEAS

Make birds in different sizes and colors. Attach thread to their bodies, and hang them from a coat hanger to make a mobile.

Blow-up Box

This classic Japanese origami design makes an interesting shape when you have finished folding it. However, if you blow into it, it inflates to make a three-dimensional box. Fold the Rocket Base first, and with a few simple folds and some clever tucks, you will soon have an origami shape with a built-in surprise!

YOU WILL NEED
Square piece of paper
8 in. x 8 in.
(20cm x 20cm)

1 Begin with the Rocket **Base.** Fold the bottom corners of the two front flaps up to the top point.

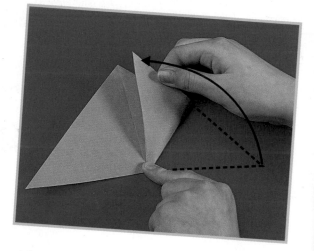

2 Turn the paper over and do the same thing on the other side.

3 Fold the two outer corners of the front flaps in to the center. Crease as shown.

 4

Turn the paper over and repeat step 3.

5

Make sure the loose points are at the top. Tuck the front two loose points into the triangle pockets as far as you can. They will not go all the way in. Turn the paper over and repeat.

Top

 6

Hold the paper lightly between your fingers and thumbs. Put the open end to your mouth and blow into the opening. The box should inflate.

FURTHER IDEAS

Make boxes in bright metallic colors and hang them up as holiday decorations, or make red lanterns for Chinese New Year.

Glossary

Base the starting place of a project

Buddhist person who follows the teaching of Buddha, an Indian religious leader from the first century B.C.E.

C.E. Common era: time after the birth of Jesus Christ

Ceremony a formal event that takes place on a special occasion

Concertina a small instrument like an accordian, the sides of which are folded in even spaces

Diagonal at an angle, often from one corner to another

Horizontal straight across

Kimono a loose, robe-like dress traditionally worn in Japan

Parallel running together with the same amount of space between all points; two horizontal lines are parallel to each other

Vertical upright, straight up and down

More Books to Read

Biddle, Steve. *Origami Safari*. New York: Tupelo Books, 1994.

LaFosse, Michael G. *Making Origami Animals Step by Step*. New York: PowerKids Press, 2002.

Urton, Andrea. *Fifty Nifty Super Animal Origami Crafts*. Chicago: Contemporary Books, 1996.

Index